"I"

OPENER

80 PARABLES

Herbert Brokering

A PERSPECTIVE II BOOK

CONCORDIA

Publishing House
St. Louis   London

CONCORDIA PUBLISHING HOUSE, ST. LOUIS, MISSOURI
CONCORDIA PUBLISHING HOUSE LTD., LONDON, E. C. 1
COPYRIGHT © 1974 CONCORDIA PUBLISHING HOUSE
PUBLISHED IN COOPERATION WITH THE BOARD OF YOUTH MINISTRY
LIBRARY OF CONGRESS CATALOG CARD
NO. 74-4912
ISBN 0-570-06472-4

MANUFACTURED IN THE UNITED STATES OF AMERICA

ENTRY POINT

A PARABLE BREAKS THROUGH THE SENSES, SEEING OLD THINGS IN A NEW WAY OR NEW THINGS IN AN OLD WAY. THE PARABLE IS STILL THE MOST POWERFUL WAY TO SEEK TRUTH, TO BE FREE.

HOW DO YOU ENTER A PARABLE? READ IT; HEAR IT. THE PARABLE DRAWS YOU IN. IT HAS THE POWER TO CATCH YOU OFF GUARD. LET IT.

HEAR IT WITH EMOTION. LET IT SPEAK TO THE SENSES. LAUGH. WINCE. OBJECT. AGREE. WONDER. LET IT UNLOCK SOMETHING IN YOU.

SOME PARABLES ARE SO IMAGINARY, SO ENCOMPASSING THAT THEY CAN BE DONE, PANTOMIMED, DANCED, ACTED. PERFORM THEM. ACT THEM OUT. DO THEM. LIVE THEM.

TALK ABOUT THE PARABLE. HEAR SEVERAL AND PICK A FAVORITE. GIVE A PARABLE TO SOMEONE — THEY MAY NEED THE MESSAGE.

COMPARE PARABLES. TALK ABOUT THEIR WORDS. FIND OUT WHAT THEY LEAVE OUT. HUDDLE WITH OTHERS OVER THEIR MEANING.

YOU MAY BE A PARABLE.

NOTICE WHEN THE PARABLE HAPPENS TO YOU. "WHY DO YOU FEEL THAT WAY?" "HAVE YOU EXPERIENCED SOMETHING LIKE THE PARABLE?"

THINKING BY ANALOGY IS CONTAGIOUS. SPREAD THE DISEASE AND TRY OUT SOME OF YOUR OWN.

JESUS TOLD PARABLES.

Once there was a minister
who wore a seed pod
to a church banquet.
They sat in the circle
and acted like they never saw it.
Someone couldn't stand it,
and she pointed to the dry boutonniere
and shouted, "It's dead!"
The man walked around the circle
and gave each person a piece.
They all went home
and planted it.
That was all he had to say.
They are still talking about it.

A PARABLE IS FOR ALL AGES

4

Once there was a boy
who lay on his back
and counted the stars.
When he was 12,
he knew the sky by heart.
He wears thick glasses now
and studies mathematics.
Now he leans over his paper
and figures out the stars.
He can do it without even
looking up.
Now his little girl
looks up at the sky.
She wishes he would do it too.

Once there was a church
that hired a toy maker for an architect.
He made church pews
so they were like crazy putty.
They could be bent
so people could see each other.
Once the people turned the pews
back to back and it worked.
There is hardly a Sunday
when they have them all
in long, straight rows.
People can make the pew
any shape they want
depending on
what they want to do.

6

Once there was a girl
who was Mary every Christmas Eve.
She reminded everyone of her,
and she didn't even
have to volunteer.
Then she met a fellow named Joe.
He was older
and good to her.
Her skin is still soft.
She cannot be Mary
this Christmas,
because she is pregnant.

A PARABLE CAN LEAD TO MIRACLES

Once there was a family
in charge of preparing
for Holy Communion.
They had it gift wrapped.
Everyone could hardly wait
while it was being opened.
When they saw the bread and wine
in side the box,
they could hardly wait to eat it.
It was Easter Sunday.
It was the best Christmas
they had ever had on Easter.

A PARABLE UNLOCKS REAL REASONS

8

Once there was a church
that had no altar.
Instead there was a circle on the floor.
Every week it was someone's turn
to be in that circle
and be an altar.
Once two boys
covered with mud
who had been fighting
stood in the circle.
They hugged each other
and smiled.
No one told them to leave.
Everyone agreed it was an altar.
There always had to be at least two
in the circle.
That was the only rule there was.

A PARABLE WELCOMES PEOPLE IN

Once there was a class
who couldn't find their pencils
and wanted to draw.
So they took a foot-long
piece of soft crocheting string.
They let it drop on their lap
in front of them just anyway it fell.
No two fell alike.
When they had dropped it,
they would look at the design
and give it a name.
They made up speeches and stories.
No one was unable to drop it
into some kind of form.
When they pick it up,
it erases without leaving a mark on their lap.
There is never a way to do it wrong.
They drop it and talk about it.

If they want to, they can help it when it drops.
Now when they do use pencils,
they buy them without erasers.
They're learning not to start over and over
but instead to go on and on.

Once there was a girl
who learned all about germs.
Her home was always sterile,
and she never drank from someone's cup.
She never missed school.
When she came to Communion,
there was just one cup.
She pretended to drink,
but her lips never touched it,
and she did not get anything to drink.
She is in excellent health
according to the medical records.

Once there was a minister
who always preached
for 20 minutes.
One day he got up and said
there was no word from the Lord today.
The people all got mad
and said they'd cut his pay.
The next Sunday
he talked for 20 minutes.
They forgave him
and promised he could stay.
Now there is a committee
that makes sure
the Word of the Lord
is said each week.
They all like him now.

Once I knew a boy
who was always sent to his room
when he was bad.
Now he is older
and has had more time to be bad.
The government has given him
a room of his own.
He is painting a picture
for a window.
He has to stay in his new room
for 140 years.
He is bad
just like they always said.

A PARABLE IS A FLASH BACK WITH A FUTURE

Once there was a boy who heard the preacher say God and Jesus a lot. His father said God when he was mad. His mother said Jesus when he got dirt on the carpet. Now he is old enough to say Jesus and God. He can say Jesus without even thinking. He can say God and not even mean it.

Once there was a boy
who liked cracking rocks.
He always thought
how he was the first to see
the inside of the rock.
He opened thousands of them.
When he was older,
he waited for the sun
to rise.
In the winter
he was the first to walk
across the new snow.
Now he is a morning milkman.
He still likes to crack things open.

Once there was a church
where once a month
they kept the doors locked.
They met on the sidewalk
and decided where they would go
to worship that day.
They went to all kinds of places
where they thought God was.
Sometimes they were chased away.
Finally they decided
to quit it.
Now they are back
inside their church building.
They haven't given up yet
and have a committee looking into the matter.
They believe God is out there
in all those places.

16

Once there was a girl
who always had her hand up,
so her teacher didn't call on her
anymore.
She is a woman now.
Once last year
she held up her hand
in a meeting,
and the leader called on her.
She was so frightened
she forgot what to say.
She is very careful
not to volunteer anymore.
She learned her lesson
a long time ago.

KEEP MOVING

A PARABLE MOLDS A MIND TO

Once there was a church
that bought a new computer.

By dialing
anyone could see and hear
what was going on in the world.
People were always busy dialing
and making connections between
the words in their church
the things happening in the world.
Someone always
dialed into her favorite disc jockey
during a hymn.
She was the only one who ever did it,
and no one says she was wrong.
In this church
people are always thinking about
what's going on outside.
Lots of young and old people go there.

Once there was a church
that had a sculptor.
He made all the Bible stories for the year
out of walnut wood.
All the people sat
between all the pieces of sculpture.
It was like being in a gallery,
and there wasn't any main part
to this room.
On the second Sunday of every month
they always sat with their eyes closed
and felt the stories
with their hands.
He said that the stories
were made to be seen
and felt.
Now the people listen better.
It is always so.

19

Once there was a church
where there were many scientists.
Their minister
was once a scientist.
He never has candles
on the altar.
He always has Bunsen burners.
All the scientists have the feeling
that their lab tables
are like altars,
and they all have a candle
in their lab.
The minister never told them to do it.
They decided this on their own.
No one ever asked them what it means.

Once there was a minister
who took up welding junk.
He is more famous for his junk sculpture
than for his sermons.
What he's most famous of all for
is helping people
not throw away
what seems to be unimportant.
In fact,
he doesn't throw anything away.
He claims it can somehow
be used
to make something valuable.
Everyone is looking twice at everything.
Also at persons.

Once there was a girl
who fell in love with the world.
She lived on it
as though it was a merry-go-round.
She ate it
as though it was delicious.
She felt it
as though it was alive.
When she grew up,
she decided to work in this world.
She thinks it is alive
and delicious.
She is a nurse
and helps people who fall off
get back on the merry-go-round.

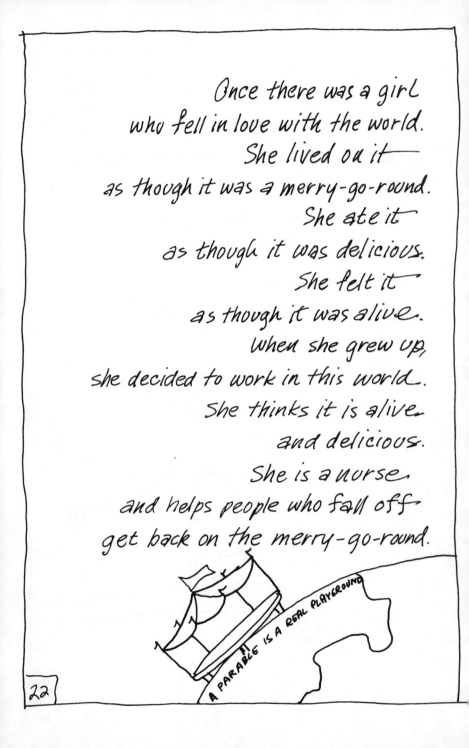

A PARABLE IS A REAL PLAYGROUND

Once there was a church
where everyone wore a mask.
They were required to do it.
Twenty minutes
was spent guessing
who was next to you.
Everyone tried hiding
as long as he could.
For 20 minutes
they took each other's masks off
and laughed about
how they had fooled each other.
Then for 20 minutes they sang songs.
That's how they spent the hour.

A PARABLE KNOWS WHEN TO STOP

23

Once there was a man
who tried to understand the Resurrection.
Once when a truck was pouring a sidewalk,
he planted a seed
in wet cement at night.
When the foundation was laid
and the building was finished,
he went to work there.
It was dedicated in the spring
when the apple blossoms were out.
He looks at the sidewalk every morning.

A PARABLE HAS DESIGNS IN IT

24

Once there was a church
that prayed for their nation
and for peace and the President
at the end of the hour.
Many people got restless
because the prayers seemed long.
Now they have a television set
in their church,
and they all pray
when the news is on.
There's one man
who turns the news on very clearly,
so everyone can see it.
All the people say the words:
Hear us and help us, good Lord.
They do it during the whole
news broadcast.
Even the ads.

Once there was a girl
who hurried home fast
through the poor part of town
so she would not get hurt.
In 10 years she hurried so fast
she never even saw it.
Now she is old enough
to take tours
into any part of the world.
She has 5,000 slides
of poverty and filth.
She is known
as a world traveler.

Once there was a church
that didn't have a cross in it.
The building committee
told them they could save
a hundred dollars that way.
Instead they each have learned
to make the sign of the cross
with their fingers.
They have learned to make
the sign
over bread and water
and over each other.
Now instead of one cross
they have hundreds of them.

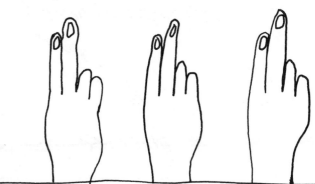

Once there was a school
where they went out a lot
to look at things.
They could not afford cameras,
so they cut holes in paper
to look through.
The large holes were for long shots.
The little holes were for closeups.
They are surprised
at how much they can see
through the holes.
The holes for closeups
wore out first.
They say they could see more
through the tiny hole.

A PARABLE OPENS WINDOWS IN SOLID WALLS

28

Once there was a clown
who became the minister.
The first thing he did
was to turn the crying room
into a dressing room.
All week long
he helps people find the face mask
they want to wear.
He is an expert at making
clown faces.
He never calls on people,
because there isn't time.
Many come to see him
to decide what faces to wear
next Sunday.

29

Once there was a teacher
who couldn't get her class
to sit close together
for the story.
So she bought a rug
just big enough for five.
All seven in her class
get on the rug for story time.
It's their favorite time
when she lays down the rug.
She suggested rugs
to the building committee.
Now they decided to get more rugs
and not build on.

Once there was a church
where the people took the offering
back home with them.
First it was collected
and brought to the altar.
After they asked God
to bless it,
they took it
and put it back into their pockets.
They mixed it up
with all their other money,
so that they couldn't tell
which was blessed
and which was not.
Then they left.
All week they spent as though
each piece was blessed
and was to be used lovingly.

31

Once there were two classes
that met in the same room.
They could not afford a wall
to separate the talking.
Someone said that sound
could be a wall.
So they brought in 10 more
classes.
Now they have
lots of voices for walls.
No one complains anymore.
They lean a little closer
to each other,
and everyone seems to like it.

Once there was a girl
who wore big hoopskirts with lace
when she was little.
Her mother always starched them,
and they stuck out.
She tried to keep them from wrinkling
and was very good at doing it.
She wanted to be a nurse
when she grew up.
She could not do it,
because she cannot get close enough
to the patients.

33

A PARABLE CAN HUMBLE A PROUD SPIRIT

Once there was a church
that got tired of the old symbols.
So they got rid of
all their triangles
and circles and doves
and sheep and crucifixes.
Now anyone can bring
any symbols they like.
There are always plenty,
and they are talked about.
Once a girl brought a broken flower,
and people tried
to keep it from dying.
Five persons helped her.
They had never seen the girl before.
The plant finally wilted.
They all thanked her
for bringing the flower.

Once there was a church
where all the flowers
were not put on the altar
but on the people.
The altar vase stood at the entrance.
Everyone who came in
received a flower
and wore it.
The flowers were always
brought by somebody.
Everyone looked ahead to giving flowers.
The name of the person
was never printed in the bulletin.
This way
everyone always thanked the person
in person.

Once there was a minister
who counseled
people breaking up.
He always had them join hands
and do a hand lock.
They pressed and pushed
against each other
in the dark
until the hand lock broke.
They would fall into each other's arms
exhausted and laughing.
Then he would always ask them,
"Do you give up?"
They answered, "I do."
Then he would pronounce them
man and wife again.

A PARABLE BRINGS PIECES BACK TOGETHER

36

Once there was a church
where the bells broke.
The church had a very tall spire.
Someone in the congregation
had a fireworks factory.
He talked the people
into letting him use the steeple
for a launching pad.
Everyone is surprised
how many people come on time
to see the fireworks
before every service begins.
Someone keeps saying
how pretty the bells were.
The children say
that they never saw them.
Now the people can hear and see
it's time for church.

Once there was a teacher
who took the children
into a library once a week.
They waved to the books,
whispered beside the dictionaries,
and tiptoed by the bird books.
They did this until they found
their favorite book.
Then they'd go to visit the author
and stay there the rest of the day
until they became an author too.
The next day they each put
their own new book
into the library.
Soon others will come
and tiptoe past the new books
and will visit them.
Then some of the books

38

A PARABLE CARRIES A WORLD BETWEEN IT LINES

will be used up for wrapping things
and for making papier-mâché animals.
Otherwise all the books would pile up so deep
there'd be no room left
for the authors to live.

Once there was a girl
who played dolls all the time.
When they would break,
her daddy fixed them
while she slept.
Now she is grown up.
She takes people's temperature
and blood pressure
when they sleep.
She remembers just how the doll felt
she used to hold.

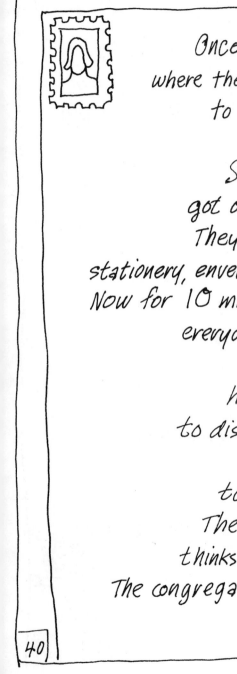

Once there was a church
where they asked a committee
to add something new
to their worship.
Some young people
got on the committee.
They suggested having
stationery, envelopes, and stamps.
Now for 10 minutes every Sunday
everyone writes letters.
The committee
had another meeting
to discuss what to do next.
They all agreed
to install telephones.
The telephone company
thinks it's a good idea.
The congregation is all for it.

Once there was a very religious person
who was a brilliant student.
He was able to do research
and to come up with convincing evidence.
During vacation he proved
to his church's Bible class back home
that the Word of God was not
what the people said it was.
He took along his term paper
to prove it.
It was so full of footnotes
there was no need to discuss it.

A PARABLE IS A REAL PLAY GROUND

41

Once there was a church
that couldn't agree.
They always kept saying
the majority rules.
So they installed a computer.
Every member can dial in
and get opinions
on anything programed in.
The computer is very busy
keeping the opinions correct.
The people never vote anymore
or have congregational meetings.
They even send favorite beliefs.
They just dial in
and get the majority opinion.
No one sees any reason
for meeting anymore.
The majority is voting to stay away.

They feel as long as they know
the majority opinion
everything is going fine.

Once there was a girl
who did everything she could
to make her doll well.
She would patch it
and paint it
and paste hair back on it.
She never hurt her doll
and always held it when it cried.
Now she is older.
She holds babies
when they cry.
She gets a new one every day
and gives it away
to its mother.

Once there was a man
who sold balloons.
A church bought 250 every Sunday.
When it was 10:45,
he would always enter
and let them fly among the people.
They would hit them and laugh.
Every time they hit a balloon,
they shouted alleluia.
That was the only thing they did:
hit and shout alleluia.
The air was full
of color and balloons,
and it was full of alleluia sounds.
It is called balloon sounds
in the bulletin.
They are trying it out this year
to see if it works.

44

Once there was a church
that believed in rhythm.
Each Sunday had a special rhythm.
The first Sunday
they did the rhythm
with their fingers and toes.
The second Sunday
they had rhythm instruments.
The third Sunday
they brought in choreographers.
The fourth Sunday
they enjoyed the rhythm of the seasons.
When there was a fifth Sunday,
they took a walk
into their city
and felt all the rhythm
of their city sounds.
Their city really has a beat.

Once there was a minister
who always went to a circus.
There were two people
on the swings
always having fun.
The man had strong arms,
and the lady
depended on them.
When he held her
and she was safe,
the minister pronounced them
man and wife.
That is where
they wanted to be married.
They still spend most of their time
in midair.

A PARABLE AWAKENS WONDER RATHER THAN WORRY

Once there was a class
who wanted to sculpture Jesus.
They had no clay or wood or marble,
so they took pumpkins
and they had their art premier
at night with candles.
One person looked at a pumpkin
until she saw it as a pumpkin pie.
She took it to a park
and ate it with her friends
on Halloween night.
Everyone who was there
thought it was a very good way
to see Jesus in a pumpkin.
Someone started the song
"Blessed be the pie that binds."
When they quit laughing, they agreed
that a pie can do it and can be a tie.

Once there was a church
that went to a circus
to learn how to worship.
In the circus there was a man
who walked
on the very high wire.
A beautiful lady
kept bowing for the people
to applaud.
They would have,
but their mouths
were full of popcorn
and their hands
held taffy and snow cones.
One day they learned to look up.
The man on the wire was glad.

Once there was a woman
who forgot who her husband was.
The two went to a church
where there was a lost-and-found room
for married people.
She stood facing one wall;
the man faced the other wall.
There he said her name,
but she did not hear her husband.
He repeated her name for 40 minutes.
If he said her name a certain way,
she knew it was her husband.
It was the way
he had said it
when they were in love.
Whenever she loses him,
they go back to the lost-and-found room
to find each other.

A PARABLE OFFERS SPACE FOR ENCOUNTERS

49

Once there was a minister
who wanted to worship
beside a popcorn popper.
They waited and waited and waited
for the first pop.
Pop.
It was loud and good news,
and they cheered.
One man whistled.
It was the first time
he heard the good news.
That was how they celebrated
Christmas Eve.
They ate popcorn all the way home.
Some think it could work on Easter.

Once there was a minister
who wore a cross
and went to where there was a war.
He got permission
to risk his life
and hold church
in the front line.
He hopped from hole to hole
hugging the soldiers.
He never stayed more than 30 seconds.
It was the only way
he could get in all the services.
One day
he held 246 services that way.
He never said a single word.

Once there was a church
on a ship.
It was a destroyer tender
that was 12 stories high
and had a space for a chapel.
The room had pulleys and ropes
and anchor chains in it.
One night someone brought in
old pews from an abandoned church
to turn the new room
into an old chapel.
One night at sea
some one put the old pews
overboard.
Now they use pillows
to sit on the floor on pulleys and ropes.
The chapel looks just like
a piece of the ship.

A PARABLE CREATES DREAMS

Once there was a minister
who had a steel helmet.
He used it to keep the sun
out of his face
and the bullets
out of his head.
He used it to cook soup,
boil water, wash his face,
and carry berries.
He can sit on it,
throw it in the air when he wins,
and kick it when he is angry.
Soldiers used the man's helmet
as an offering plate,
a plate for bread,
and a cup for Communion.
When Christmas comes,
he will use it as a manger.

Once there was a church
where they couldn't find the Bible
one Sunday.
The minister asked if anyone
had good news from the Lord.
No one admitted having any,
so they all started leaving.
One man said his wife
had just had a baby this morning.
The people decided that this
wasn't a word from the Lord,
and they went home.
The man stayed for a whole hour.
He was sure that was good news
from the Lord.

Once there was a teacher
who took a year off from spelling
and took up talking and looking.
They all looked and looked
and told what they saw.
It took her very long to prepare.
They always looked at something
just going around a corner,
through a door, or into a cloud.
All year they saw tails
and wings and wheels and leaves.
They had to guess
what animal or machine or plant or person
it belonged to.
This was a very important way
in which to put together their eyes and mouth.
Now they are ready to spell again
for awhile.

Once there was a church
where the organ broke.
So they opened their windows
and listened.
They heard the clapping of thunder,
the transmissions of trucks,
the beat of jumping ropes,
the swaying of leaves,
the rubbing of branches,
the drone of the fan,
the walking of women,
the running of boys,
the moving of traffic,
and the whistling of wind.
Every Sunday they do this.
They are thinking of not replacing
the organ for a while.

Once there was a church
that wanted mosaics put in
like their neighboring church.
They could not afford it,
so they formed a committee.
Now on the first day of the week
everyone gets a magic marker.
For 15 minutes
they draw graffiti feelings on the walls.
No one mentions mosaics anymore.
The neighboring church
is putting a plastic coating
to protect their mosaics against vandals.

Once there was a teacher
who wanted to get more nerve.
So he thumbed his nose
at his books.
Now he is able to do
anything he wants to with books.
Whenever the books get him down,
he thumbs his nose.
He can even work up nerve
during class
without anyone knowing
he's doing it.
He is learning to be stronger than books.
Very few books frighten him
anymore.

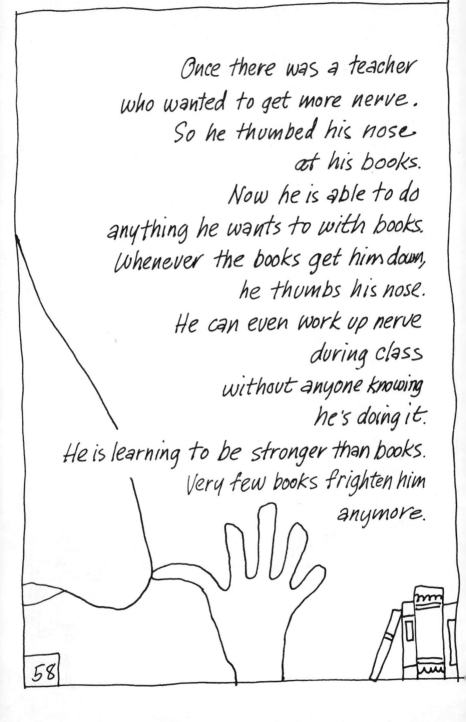

Once there was a priest
and four nuns
who loaded the jeep
with Coke and cookies
and took them into the firing line.
The men were glad they came,
and ate and drank.
As the jeep left, the chaplain said,
"Jesus is here."
A soldier said, "No."
The priest said, "Yes."
Everyone believed the priest
and cheered.
The men remember
Jesus surprised them that way.

X A PARABLE EVOKES IMAGES BY WHICH PEOPLE SURVIVE IN A HOSTILE WORLD.

Once there was a teacher
who never complained.
Whenever there was a problem,
she made it her lesson.
That's all she did
was solve problems.
Once she substituted
in a class that didn't tell
their problems.
So she ran out of things to do.
She was glad to get back
to her class
with so many problems.
They were glad to see her,
and there was so much to do.

PROBLEMS   PROBLEMS   PROBLEMS
PROBLEMS   PROBLEMS   PROBLEMS
PROBLEMS   PROBLEMS   PROBLEMS
PROBLEMS   PROBLEMS   PROBLEMS
PROBLEMS   PROBLEMS   PROBLEMS

Once there was a girl
who wanted to be a minister
when she grew up.
Everyone told her to stop saying it
because it was silly,
so she did.
She became one anyway
and didn't tell the people.
She washes feet,
says the people's names,
tries to get Sundays off,
sometimes works all night,
and helps the people go to sleep.
She can make a bedroom
feel like Communion.
She is very pretty.
When she was ordained,
they gave her a white cap.

Once there was a teacher
who was an author.
On the first day
she taught everyone in the class
to be an author too.
If something sounded special
as if it hadn't ever been said,
she'd say, "Author, author."
Everyone would join in.
Sometimes they'd memorize the sentence
or make it into a poster
or give it a tune and sing it.
Whenever they write papers,
they put each other into the footnotes.
Some of them are quoted a lot.
Everyone tries to get
into the footnotes
with lots of op cits.

Once there was a girl
who believed in miracles
and helped butterflies get started over.
Once she helped a baby bird until it died.
Once she helped a caterpillar be grateful.
Now she is older,
and she works with the doctor.
They make things come back to life.

〰〰〰〰〰 A PARABLE IS A SIGNS OF STRUGGLE

Once there was a church
where people came
who had trouble loving others.
They practiced by holding hands
and saying yes, yes, yes,
to each other.
They took turns saying it
until everybody was sure
they heard someone say yes.

Once there was a teacher
who knew lots of stories,
and they were all true.
The story she told best
was always the one that was just going on
or had just happened,
and the class was always in it.
Whenever they were learning,
they talked about what was happening,
so that it was a story.
It was always the only story
all of them could remember,
and they knew it by heart.
Whenever things aren't going well
and they want to learn,
they think about the story that is going on,
and then what is happening
is important.

Once there was a school,
and all the furniture burned.
The people were too poor to replace it.
Months later they even forgot
how desks used to cut them in half
and hide more than half of their body
while they were learning.
Now when they learn,
they do it with their whole body
and not only with the top part.
It took them all year
to get used to learning that way.
Their teacher doesn't only
look at their faces
when she teaches them.
There is no front to the room anymore.
They can even learn sideways,
or back to back.

Once there was a class
who didn't know what orange was,
so they put on orange hats,
made an orange box with an orange hole in it,
and ate orange candy on an orange rug.
They played there until night
and waved to an orange moon
while they smelled orange peels.
Now when someone says that orange is a color,
they know that orange is also sticky
and it squirts.
One boy played orange
on his plastic sweet potato
and said he did it
by spelling orange blue.
That's because he thinks music is blue.
The next color they're going to discover
is blue.

When they do, orange will be in there too
because of the boy
who played orange with blue notes
on his red-and-white sweet potato.

Once there was a boy
who drew his first picture
when he was three.
Everyone asked him
what it was.
He kept doing it over,
hoping they would be able
to tell what it was.
It is the only picture
he has drawn so far.
Someday he hopes to finish it.
When he does,
he wants to draw his second picture.

Once there was a teacher
who wanted to give her class Bibles.
While they had an outing,
she carried them in a package all day.
Everyone asked her to tell
what was in the package
because they thought it was their present.
It was, and she opened it
when they were drinking hot chocolate
while sitting in a hay barn singing songs.
When she broke the string,
all the books fell into the hay.
Someone laughed and said
this book was like Jesus in hay.
The teacher could hardly believe
what she had heard,
and said it was absolutely true.
Then she gave each one a Bible

and a piece of hay
while they sang a Christmas song.
Every time they go to learn,
they do it in a way they won't ever forget.
The only reason they even repeat a lesson
is because they're telling someone
what happened when they learned.

Once there was a teacher
who liked games.
He would always cut up the book
and put it on cards.
He would shuffle them
and play the lesson like a game.
Everyone always
got part of the book.
Everyone was always in the lesson.

Once there was a teacher
who collected junk and scrap pieces
from desk drawers and wastebaskets.
Every semester he'd shake the box
and pour it into a pile
in the middle of the class.
For 30 minutes
they'd organize all the pieces
into the shape of a cross
or some other shape
with their eyes shut.
It helped them with their feeling,
so when they looked at it later,
they'd see more how they felt
about all the different pieces.
Every time they do it,
they know why blind people
know so many different kinds of things

and go so slow when they learn.
There's so much there.
There is a blind person in the class.
He is the teacher.
He really knows what he is doing.

Once there was a group of people
who added up their ages.
They were only 20 persons,
but their years totaled so many
that if they were laid end to end
they would reach the time of Christ.
Now they don't act as though
someone in another city
should do all their thinking.
It didn't happen though
until they were willing to admit their ages
and how many years they had lived.

A PARABLE COMES WHEN ITS TOO PAINFUL FOR
ANYTHING ELSE.

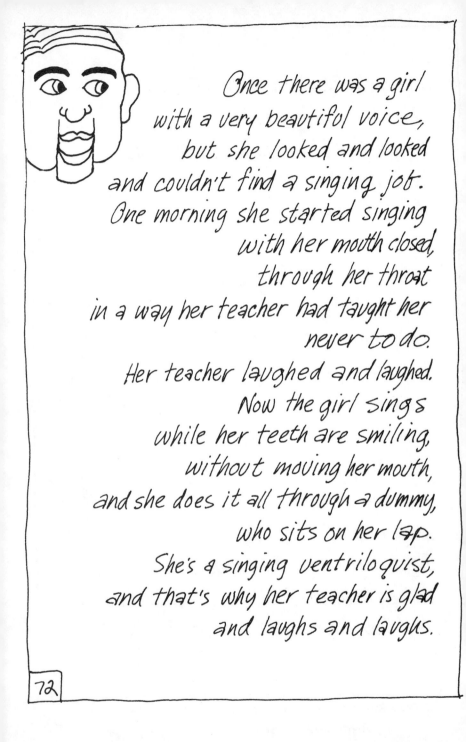

Once there was a girl
with a very beautiful voice,
but she looked and looked
and couldn't find a singing job.
One morning she started singing
with her mouth closed,
through her throat
in a way her teacher had taught her
never to do.
Her teacher laughed and laughed.
Now the girl sings
while her teeth are smiling,
without moving her mouth,
and she does it all through a dummy,
who sits on her lap.
She's a singing ventriloquist,
and that's why her teacher is glad
and laughs and laughs.

The dummy keeps singing
that he was a tree
who grew south of Jerusalem.

Once there was a girl
who was born with a hole in her heart.
When she was old enough,
they sewed it shut.
Ever since
her heart is very open.
Some healthy people
wish they had had open-heart surgery
to open their hearts more.
They think the operation did it.
It was her mother
who really did it.
The doctor only sewed it
the way it was.

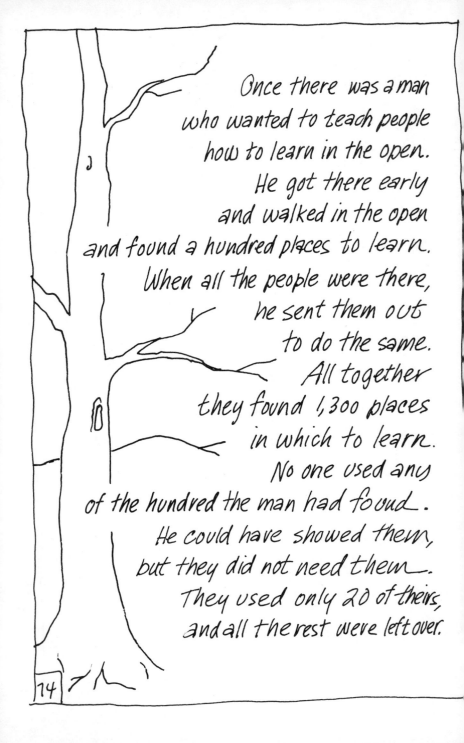

Once there was a man
who wanted to teach people
how to learn in the open.
He got there early
and walked in the open
and found a hundred places to learn.
When all the people were there,
he sent them out
to do the same.
All together
they found 1,300 places
in which to learn.
No one used any
of the hundred the man had found.
He could have showed them,
but they did not need them.
They used only 20 of theirs,
and all the rest were left over.

74

Once there was a church
that ran out of things to do.
They had done all the hymns
and said all the prayers
over and over.
They knew the festivals by heart
and could recite psalms
without looking or thinking.
So they decided to celebrate
the only thing left:
Each other.
Every week they celebrate one person.
So many people are joining.
It seems they'll never get done
with what they're doing.

Once there was a girl
who had a special speech defect.
When she was older,
she went to a modeling school
to learn how to be more graceful.
While doing it
her speech defect fit in
with the new way she walked.
She dances beautifully,
and those who know her
especially like the way she talks.
Now she teaches dancing to a professor
of languages
who thinks he was born
with a dancing defect.

A PARABLE OPENS DOORS BETWEEN FEELING
AND THOUGHTS

Once there was a girl
who never went to school
after she was 12.
She had learned enough
to have two Ph.D.'s
before she was 30,
but there was no university
in the whole country
that would take all the credits she had.
Besides, they had to admit,
they don't even have courses
in what she learned.
If they ever did,
she'd be a professor.
She's really glad she asked them
because now she doesn't think
she only got to the fifth grade.

CERTIFICATE

Once there was a man
who was given a beautiful empty bag as a gift.
All he had to do
was to fill it with anything he liked.
He thought he did'nt have time to do this,
so he gave back the bag.

Once there was a congregation
who wanted to know how to read
their statistical report.
They wrote up a true story
of what was happening to them.
When they checked it,
all the statistics were in the story.
Everyone can read the story
and everyone is in it.
They wrote it together
when no one was looking.

4
5
3 4 6 5 2 1
7
8
9

Once there was a girl
who always started over
when she made mistakes
on her violin.
When she was 30,
she was famous.
Many people came to hear her.
One night she gave a concert,
and everyone was there.
She made a mistake,
and so she started over.
Everyone got up when she was done,
and they applauded for 10 minutes.
She was glad
she had learned
how to start over.

Once there was a girl looking for resources. When she read about one and ordered it, she found she already had it. She was so glad that she didn't even bother to send it back.

Once there was a church that was looking for better questions. Now every time they get together, they have the feeling something important is going to happen. If it ever didn't, someone would be sure to ask why.

A PARABLE IS FOR ALL AGES